Women
RELIGIOUS,
Women
DEACONS

Questions and Answers

Phyllis Zagano

Paulist Press
New York / Mahwah, NJ

Cover image by Marisha/Shutterstock.com
Cover and book design by Lynn Else

Library of Congress Cataloging-in-Publication Data
Names: Zagano, Phyllis, author.
Title: Women religious, women deacons : questions and answers / Phyllis Zagano.
Description: New York ; Mahwah, NJ : Paulist Press, 2022. | Summary: "This book is for anyone interested in the question of women religious and women deacons, comprising five essays, each with questions for discussion"—Provided by publisher.
Identifiers: LCCN 2021055248 (print) | LCCN 2021055249 (ebook) | ISBN 9780809156122 (paperback) | ISBN 9780809187720 (ebook)
Subjects: LCSH: Women clergy. | Women in the Catholic Church. | Deaconesses—Catholic Church. | Nuns. | Monasticism and religious orders for women.
Classification: LCC BX1912.2 .Z346 2022 (print) | LCC BX1912.2 (ebook) | DDC 262.14082—dc23/eng/20220110
LC record available at https://lccn.loc.gov/2021055248
LC ebook record available at https://lccn.loc.gov/2021055249

ISBN 978-0-8091-5612-2 (paperback)
ISBN 978-0-8091-8772-0 (e-book)

Published by Paulist Press
997 Macarthur Boulevard
Mahwah, New Jersey 07430
www.paulistpress.com

Printed and bound in the
United States of America

*For all the women who wish
to follow Saint Phoebe in ministry*

Contents

Foreword

Only in 2016 did most religious begin to think about women in the diaconate. In that year, at their triennial meeting in Rome, the members of the International Union of Superiors General (UISG) asked Pope Francis to establish a commission to study the question. The sisters noted that many of their number were already doing diaconal work. Why could they not be ordained?

The years prior to that meeting saw a growing number of publications on the topic. Dr. Phyllis Zagano's books as well as publications by Professor Gary Macy and Deacon William Ditewig taught me, and I suspect many others, that there were women deacons in the early church and up to the twelfth century in the West. Somehow, that history never appeared in all my theological and church history coursework.

Today, as a Dominican woman religious devoted to *veritas* and preaching, I realize that I, and so many other religious, have been engaged in diaconal work all along: women religious lead groups; we train and educate various people; and we serve the poor in a myriad of ways.

With *Women Religious, Women Deacons* Dr. Zagano provides a roadmap to a synodal process for women religious, many of whom belong to institutes initially formed to minister in a diaconal manner. When cloistered life was the rule for women, noncloistered institutes were created to perform charitable works, to meet the pressing needs of the people. As the needs grew, so did the many apostolic institutes that reached out to the poor and those in need and that also supported and educated immigrants far from home.

In these chapters, Dr. Zagano creates space for women religious to discern the questions surrounding the possibility of women religious being ordained. How would institutes train or incorporate women deacons? Should they? Would women religious ordained as deacons enhance their ministries and works?

An ordained person is a cleric. An ordained woman religious, while ordained by a bishop, would be missioned by her superior. Unlike a secular woman deacon—married or celibate—who would be assigned by her bishop to a particular ministry, the religious woman ordained as a deacon would be available for assignment only by her superior. How would an institute determine the diaconal works an individual sister would best perform?

Would ordained members disrupt community life? It is my belief that at this time in history there would not arise a clerical distinction between an ordained and nonordained member of a religious institute. As Dr. Zagano notes, even with deacons as professed members, both lay and ordained sisters would be eligible to be elected as general superiors.

As people around the world raise the issue of the restoration of women to the diaconate, these chapters and study questions support the understanding of and need for women—

including women religious—to be restored to ordained diaconal ministry should their vocations encompass such.

As the synod process unfolds, this book will provide both learning and conversation aids for fruitful discussions about needs of the church in the twenty-first century. Religious have historically stepped up to serve the church. We are today called to encounter, listen, and discern the church's needs, the needs of the people of God. Religious have historically lived in communion, participation, and mission. It is important to expand our charisms into the future of possibility.

Donna L. Ciangio, OP
Chancellor, Archdiocese of Newark

Acknowledgments

This book is based on the five-part series "Women Religious, Women Deacons: Questions and Answers," which ran in the *Global Sisters Report* between January 14 and February 11, 2021. It includes questions useful for personal consideration or group discussion and discernment written and reviewed by Donna L. Ciangio, OP, Colleen Gibson, SSJ, and Irene M. Kelly, RSHM, along with questions garnered from the February 12, 2021, "Witness and Grace" Zoom conversation among *GSR* editor Gail DeGeorge, Colleen Gibson, SSJ, and Phyllis Zagano. Thanks are due to the above, and all who helped with this project, including Teresa Malcolm, Anne P. Myers, SSJ, and Regina M. Scaringella, OP, as well as Bob Byrns, Paul McMahon, and the many others who make Paulist Press the fine Catholic publishing house it is.

Introduction

In May 2016, Pope Francis responded to a question posed at the triennial assembly of the International Union of Superiors General (UISG): If women religious are already performing the many ministries of deacons, why not form a commission to study the restoration of women to the diaconate?

The pope responded immediately, naming twelve scholars the following August to the Commission for the Study of the Diaconate of Women, who met in Rome four times and returned a report by June 2018. The pope gave a portion of the report to the UISG leadership at their May 2019 assembly. It has not yet been published.

Then, in October 2019, at the Synod of Bishops for the Pan-Amazon Region, the same question arose: If nearly two-thirds of parish groupings are managed by women religious there, why not install women as lectors and acolytes, and share the synod's support of women deacons with the commission?

Again, Francis agreed, saying he would recall the commission, perhaps adding two or three new members. Then, in April 2020, he named an entirely new group to study the question.

This second commission began work in September 2021. It will be the fourth or fifth iteration of commission study of the same topic since the early 1970s. None recommended against women deacons.

Specific questions arise when considering women religious in the ordained diaconate. In the Orthodox churches, for example, the history of women deacons is not debated. Women, especially monastic women, are and have been ordained as deacons. The Latin-rite West, however, has debated the issue for hundreds of years. Furthermore, the modern commissions uniformly agreed that women deacons existed in the early church, East and West: some women deacons were religious, others were married; some were single, others were widows.

Now, it was the UISG that brought the question directly to the pope. Even so, not all women religious seek ordination as deacons, and rightly so. The specific vocation to the ordained diaconate is not a replacement for religious life, nor is it a replacement for the priesthood. But, just as with the priesthood, the ordained diaconate can coexist with religious life.

While there is no guarantee that Pope Francis will change canon law to allow women to be restored to this ordained ministry, this book examines the questions most often raised by women religious about the possibility of women religious being ordained as deacons or of women deacons joining religious institutes and orders.

FOR REFLECTION

1. What do deacons do?
2. Do you think the diaconate is an important office in the church today?
3. How might the role of women deacons expand our vision of church and service?

1

Why Women Religious as Deacons?

Why did the International Union of Superiors General (UISG) ask for a study of women deacons? Women religious are not women deacons, but many women religious undertake the tasks and duties of the diaconate. The UISG sisters pointed this out quite clearly to Pope Francis when they asked for the study—and by implication his consideration—of women deacons in 2016, and their comments were seconded by the Synod for the Amazon in 2019.

Throughout history we can locate specific times and cultures in which religious institutes formed to meet the pressing, and diaconal, needs of the people of God. Why? During the Middle Ages the diaconate became increasingly ceremonial as the priestly class took over the administration of the church's treasure. Ministry to the people gradually, but increasingly, became centered on sacrament and ceremony. The diaconate faded and, apart from a ceremonial office, virtually disappeared by the twelfth century.

The Council of Trent (1543–63) unsuccessfully attempted to restore the diaconate as a permanent ministerial vocation. Throughout the ensuing centuries, the absence of a functioning diaconate contributed to the development of apostolic religious life to meet the needs of the poor and disenfranchised.

The exponential growth of religious orders and institutes over the centuries between Trent and the Second Vatican Council demonstrates the ongoing needs of the people of God. Women's apostolic institutes especially were formed to meet specific needs at specific times in specific territories, although many expanded beyond their founding locations to take up works farther afield.

However, as apostolic institutes developed and grew, they were largely distinct from the diocesan structure, and especially separate from diocesan finances. In fact, apostolic religious institutes—both papal and diocesan—are primarily self-funded.

Those orders and institutes of men that include clerics find opportunities for their members' employment within diocesan structures, especially parishes, in addition to their self-initiated works of education, social service, and charitable endeavors.

However, apostolic institutes of women most often develop and run their ministries independently. While many women religious can and do find employment within diocesan entities, they are employees without any ministerial connection to, or faculties from, the bishop. They may work within diocesan structures, especially school systems, but their pay in too many countries is often minimal and, unlike parish priests, they are not provided free room and board. Furthermore, as members of diocesan or papal institutes, women are not guaranteed any support from the bishop.

Canon law states that married deacons "who devote themselves completely to ecclesiastical ministry deserve remuneration by which they are able to provide for the support of themselves and their families" (Can. 281 §3). The key words here are "completely to ecclesiastical ministry." Deacons who are part-time employees or volunteers in a diocesan entity or parish are expected to maintain themselves and their families through their personal employment.

Different dioceses present different remuneration schedules for deacons, but many offer retreats and educational gatherings in addition to reimbursement for their ministerial expenses. In many dioceses, any money received for witnessing marriages, performing baptisms, and officiating at funerals is to be returned to the parish.

But women religious provide their own funds for their retreats and educational gatherings, as well as for their personal needs and those of their communities.

Beyond the question of remuneration, in asking for consideration of restoring women to the ordained diaconate, UISG members recognized that clerical status carries with it the more formal connection to the sacramental and ministerial life of the church. Secular women ministers, pastoral associates, catechists, and diocesan employees, including those of the various Orthodox churches, have recognized the same. Hence, the calls for the restoration of women to the ordained diaconate have become increasingly urgent in the past fifty years.

Coincidentally, over the past fifty years there has been a combination of local and universal synods discussing the question of women deacons, along with repeated iterations of papal commissions and of subcommissions of the International Theological Commission.

Therefore, the May 2016 UISG request for a commission to study women deacons must be viewed against the backdrop of the growing trajectory of formal and informal discussion informed by questions of justice for those ministering as well as for those being ministered to. The discussion never centered directly on women religious, nor on women religious becoming deacons, until the UISG membership presented the idea to Pope Francis.

The most pressing question that the UISG presented is rooted in fact: Because women religious are performing so many diaconal tasks and duties, why can they not be ordained as deacons? Their logic is the same as that of the Diaconate Circles formed in Germany after World War II that eventually became the impetus for restoring the diaconate as a permanent vocation for secular men—married or celibate.

In 1951, a group of young social workers formed the first Diaconate Circle in Freiburg, Germany. They published "Working Papers" from 1952 until 1966, by which time the Second Vatican Council was seriously considering restoring the diaconate as a permanent vocation.

During the intervening years, other Diaconate Circles formed in Germany, France, Austria, and Latin America, and joined together to form the International Diaconate Circle, based in Freiburg. In 1962, they petitioned the bishops of Vatican II, asking that the diaconate be restored as a permanent vocation.

When the question of restoring the diaconate as a permanent vocation arose, some council members voiced objections like those now voiced against restoring women to the diaconate.

Two cardinals, Cologne Archbishop Josef Frings (1887–1978) and French Cardinal André-Damien-Ferdinand Jullien (1882–1964), then-dean emeritus of the Roman Rota, the church's "supreme court," expressed concern as to how the restoration would affect the lay apostolate. As with the question of women and the diaconate today, the point that many diaconal functions were being performed by laypersons was advanced then as a reason not to ordain men to the permanent vocation of deacon.

Yet then, as now, the fact that many laypersons are performing diaconal ministry is reason enough to identify more people—male and female—who may have vocations to the order of deacon. As Vatican II noted, these ministers would be strengthened by the grace and charism of diaconal ordination, a point that had been stressed by Cardinal Leo Joseph Suenens (1904–96), then-archbishop of Mechelen-Brussels, and which continues to be part of the continuing discussion.

FOR REFLECTION

1. Why do you think the International Union of Superiors General (UISG) requested another study of women deacons? Do you agree with the UISG request for another study of women deacons? Why or why not?

2. Is there a distinction between the charitable ministry of women religious and of deacons? If vowed religious took over the charitable duties of deacons during the Middle Ages, do you think ordaining women, including women religious,

as deacons could have a similar benefit for the church?

3. Religious institutes manage many charitable institutions outside and within diocesan structures. How do you think ordaining women religious as deacons could benefit your institute or order?

4. The UISG stated that women religious are already doing diaconal work. Do you know of women religious whose ministries would be enhanced and strengthened by their ordination as deacons?

5. The Diaconate Circles formed in Europe following World War II laid the groundwork for Vatican II's reestablishment of the permanent diaconate for men. Are there any groups or individuals who are studying or discerning the diaconate as a permanent vocation for women today? How might their efforts affect the consideration of women deacons?

2

What about Ordained Women Religious?

While discussion about women in the diaconate has historically been truncated—even squashed—within the Vatican, the request of UISG in 2016 and the recommendation of the Amazon Synod in 2019 are both evidence of the genuine need for a diaconal ministry by women ordained to such service. The point is not to allow women religious and other women merely to take on more functions but rather to allow the church to recognize them as women, as religious, and as pastoral ministers and, should they find within themselves the vocation to the diaconate, as ordained clerics.

Of course, the effort has never been about "clericalization." More readily, the effort is to connect the present ministries of religious and secular women to the ministry of the bishop, and thereby secure it in union with the whole church. The question of restoring women, including women religious, to the ordained diaconate moves beyond the notion of their tasks and duties, beyond the "functions" they would more clearly assume. For women religious, such restoration includes identifying these women ministers as who they are: as religious, surely, but also as deacons, if they are so called.

Even so, the functions are an important part of the puzzle because, especially in mission territories, women religious are already performing the functions of deacons. But there are other things laypersons cannot do; a woman ordained as a deacon would be able to preach the homily at a given Mass and serve as single judge in a canonical proceeding—just two among other tasks and duties restricted to clerics.

For opponents, the troubling problem with ordained women—religious or secular, it must be stated—is that they would be vested and part of the celebration of the Mass. While the deacon at Mass proclaims the Gospel, and can preach if invited, the deacon has other liturgical functions within the sacred celebration.

In fact, the deacon's tasks are many. In addition to processing with the celebrating priest, addressing the assembly, proclaiming the Gospel, and preaching, the deacon prays the universal prayer and dismisses the congregation at the end of the celebration.

However, most distressing to misogynists is the fact that the deacon ministers the chalice at the altar. In other words, the deacon mixes the water and the wine for the sacrifice, fills the chalice, and hands it to the priest. At the showing of the consecrated elements, the deacon elevates the chalice. The deacon also assists with the distribution of communion, most formally with the administration of the chalice.

While in many territories the presence of women at the altar as lectors or acolytes is not in the least upsetting to the people of God, pockets of fear are fed by clerics and others for whom the very sight of a woman at the altar is sacrilegious. For these people, allowing a woman to touch the sacred vessels, let alone mix the water and the wine for the sacrifice, is scandalous.

Such attitudes reach back into the history of ancient blood taboos, many of which are maintained in closed cultures today. Consider, for example, menstruation huts and the taboos regarding men touching women or of women touching objects.

But the point of ordaining women religious, particularly those who have the care of parishes and parish groupings in many areas of the world, is to enhance, even professionalize, their various ministries. Again, however, the diaconate is not necessary for all women religious, especially and including those who work in mission territories. The diaconate does not replace religious life. The diaconate is necessary for those women religious for whom it is a genuine vocation, distinct from their vocation and identity as a religious.

There are approximately forty-seven thousand men, mostly married, who serve as deacons within diocesan and parish structures throughout the world. Many bishops have warmed to the idea of including women among their ranks. Recall that it was the International Union of Superiors General that asked Pope Francis to consider the ordination of women to the diaconate. Their request included the fact that women religious in many territories were already doing the work of deacons. So, why not ordain them?

The UISG sisters pressed this point very specifically. The fact that they were already performing diaconal ministry potentially underscores their disconnect from the hierarchical church. The sisters who are working in parish structures may be employed by the parish, or their work may be missioner work as part of the charism of their institutes.

The diaconal works of women religious (e.g., medical clinics, food banks, educational initiatives) are largely self-funded. Hence, the request of the UISG strikes at the heart of the diaconal vocation and office in the church. It underscores the need for bishops and parishes to provide for the poor with diocesan resources, not replacing the many organizational works of women religious, but complementing them.

The unspoken question concerns the relationship between the deacon and the bishop. Historically, the deacon served as the diocesan bishop's "right hand," and women deacons functioned in that capacity both literally and figuratively. They anointed ill women as well as female candidates for baptism. One woman deacon, Anna, is remembered as the treasurer of Rome.

But as the ordained diaconate of women was increasingly repressed into abbeys and monasteries, its functions became increasingly, if not wholly, ceremonial, as did the functions of male deacons. Even so, within the abbeys and monasteries, women deacons were still needed to minister to ill sisters and to lead community prayer. Women consecrated as abbesses, often also ordained as deacons, still proclaimed the gospel and preached to their sisters.

Candidates for the diaconate must be installed and minister as lectors and acolytes prior to diaconal ordination. In

2021, Pope Francis changed canon 230 §1 to allow women to be installed. There is no church finding that women cannot be ordained as deacons, only the assumption that canon 1024 ("A baptized male alone receives sacred ordination validly.") applies to the diaconate as well as to the priesthood. However, when this law began to be codified, for the most part only men preparing for priesthood were ordained as subdeacons, then as deacons. The revised Book 6 of the Code of Canon Law appears to include the diaconate in its delicts, but church opinion on the matter (*Inter Insigniores*, 1976, and *Ordinatio Sacerdotalis*, 1994) solely addresses the question of women priests. Is the church capable of seeing women—both secular and religious women—as bearers of the gospel and as icons of Christ?

FOR REFLECTION

1. How do you define *clericalism*? Do you think that the ordination of women as deacons would add to the church's problem of clericalism?

2. Is it important for women parochial ministers to have an official office in the church?

3. Is it beneficial for the church to allow women to be vested and preach during public celebrations of the Eucharist? Who benefits? How?

4. In many places ancient taboos against women still exist along with notions that women are inferior. In your experience, how have you or others overcome such prejudice? Have you been

affected by any misogynistic views and acts of clerics?

5. Do you think there are segments of the church that still consider women "unclean"? Can these beliefs be overcome? How valid are the fears and concerns of those opposed to women serving as deacons?

6. Aside from a ceremonial role at the altar, how could women answering the call to the diaconate enhance the pastoral life of a parish?

3

Who
Could Be
the General
Superior?

It is a documented fact that women, including some members of abbeys and monasteries, were ordained as deacons. The misconception that the ordination of women deacons was "only" the ceremonial appointment of an abbess ignores both their sacramental diaconal ordinations and their abbatial consecrations, which gave them jurisdictional powers and authority. In some liturgies, the two nominations are collapsed, but without question, some abbesses were ordained as deacons and had territorial jurisdictional authority equivalent to that of bishops within their abbey and monastery territories.

While some abbesses, and deacon-abbesses, maintained ecclesiastical jurisdiction over their territorial abbeys for many centuries, their authority was overruled in the nineteenth century by Pope Pius IX.

Other questions of jurisdiction arise within any discussion of clerics in religious orders and institutes. History aside, the ordination of a woman permanently incorporated in a religious institute or order presents many questions, because ordination introduces a cleric into the institute or order. Mixed clerical and lay religious institutes and orders of men ordain members as priests, some include deacons, and have lay members (brothers). Most, if not all, are willing to incorporate secular priests, and some men's institutes steadfastly remain lay.

Ordaining a woman religious would, technically, at least, make the women's institute or order mixed, that is, comprising both clerical and lay members. The following questions arise: Would the major superior of the mixed institute or order of women religious need to be a deacon? Would only members who are deacons be eligible for election?

Current canon law requires that the major superior of a mixed clerical and lay institute or order of men must be a priest with the assumption that all or, at least, some of its clerical members are priests. While discussions have been undertaken between religious orders of men and the Congregation for Institutes of Consecrated Life and Societies of Apostolic Life, the canonical requirement is that the general superior must be a priest, and any matters pertaining to priest members must be attended to by priests.

Despite historical evidence of lay jurisdiction in men's orders, the canon stymies any change. For example, today, the election of a deacon or lay member as the men's general superior generally cannot go forward unless he is willing to be ordained as priest. Such is a rare event, generally occurring within monasteries in the Benedictine tradition.

In 1996, Pope John Paul II's post-synodal apostolic exhortation *Vita Consecrata* promised a commission to examine the apparent collision between a founder's original vision of common brotherhood among members of some men's religious orders that now comprise priests and nonpriests. There is no evidence such a commission ever met despite the fact that, as John Paul II wrote in the apostolic exhortation, "the Synod Fathers expressed the hope that in these Institutes all the Religious would be recognized as having equal rights and obligations, with the exception of those which stem from Holy Orders."

Because no commission has been formed, no recommendation has been made. However, some orders of men, notably the Capuchin Franciscans, have elected lay brothers as provincial superiors and have had those elections approved. At least one instance in the United States of such an election demonstrates the willingness for Pope Francis, if not the Vatican congregation for religious, to bend, if only a little. The Capuchin Province of St. Conrad (Mid-America), headquartered in Denver, elected Br. Mark Schenk as provincial minister in 2019. To be validated, the election required a direct dispensation from Pope Francis, which he granted. The province was required to appoint a priest vicar for priestly matters.

Does this question apply to women's orders and institutes? Canonists tend to think not, because a woman religious ordained as deacon would, quite simply, not be a priest. An individual ordained to the diaconate is a cleric, but the individual ordained as deacon is canonically distinct from an individual ordained to the priesthood. The distinction is such that the inclusion of women deacons with women's religious orders and institutes would appear to make little, if any, difference.

In addition to the question of who can serve as general superior, one question that often arises is whether the deacon-member would be responsible to the bishop.

Before incorporating women deacons or sending professed members for diaconal studies, the general superior of the order or institute would need to determine—in consultation with her council—whether the order or institute wishes to take on a "mixed" character, should the member be ordained. Some religious institutes of men, notably the Edmund Rice Christian Brothers (the Irish Christian Brothers), have formally rejected the notion of including clerics. Should the woman's institute determine its charism is specifically lay, then the question of lay or clerical leadership becomes moot.

However, should the women's institute determine that it wishes to incorporate women deacons or to place its members on the path toward diaconal ordination, the question of authority arises. Today, most deacons are secular men (most married) incardinated within dioceses. The major superior of a woman religious would be the only person who could grant her permission for ordination, but would the member's ordination conflict in any way with her vow of obedience within the institute?

Such is a potential red herring, and one easily dismissed. The member, no matter her lay or clerical status, belongs to the institute.

The question then arises: Who would mission the member? Clearly, the missioning of a member, whether of a diocesan or pontifical institute, would remain with the woman's general superior. As with any assignment, the member's work within a diocesan entity, and sometimes even within a diocese, would need the diocesan bishop's approval, but he would not be able to "order" a sister to work in a particular ministry.

Separately, however, a sister-deacon who is missioned by her superior to work as a deacon in a particular location must have faculties from the diocesan bishop. Interestingly, there is lingering evidence within the Code of Canon Law regarding preaching faculties within women's convents, and the argument can be made that only the woman's general superior can grant these faculties within her territory.

In any event, for ministerial assignments, the situation is analogous to those for any other religious cleric. Individual faculties from the diocesan bishop are required for ordinary and regular ministry in any given diocese. However, the missioning of the member remains within the purview of the institute.

Even so, many other questions arise regarding the prospect of women religious becoming deacons.

FOR REFLECTION

1. Do you think your institute (or order) would undertake discussions and discern whether to allow members to be ordained or include women already ordained as deacons?

2. Understanding that the diaconate is not the priesthood, do you have any concerns about governance and jurisdiction within your institute should it decide to allow members to be ordained or include women already ordained as deacons?

3. What do you think of having both lay and ordained members in your institute? Would having a mixed institute of clerics and lay be an advantage or disadvantage? Why or why not?

4. Sisters already minister outside their own institutions with the permission of the diocesan bishop of the locale. In theory, the diocesan bishop cannot order a sister to work in a specific ministry. Do you agree that this would still be the case if a sister were ordained as deacon?

4

Would Diaconal Ordination Co-opt Women's Religious Life?

Much has been written about women's religious institutes being "outside the system" and thereby freer to act on behalf of the people of God. Significant discussion within and without these institutes echoes the thought of the second sister to speak to Pope Francis at the UISG triennial meeting in May 2019, informing him that she was not interested in ordination. For various reasons, many women religious do not wish to be associated with the clergy and argue that ordaining or incorporating women clerics—deacons or priests—as members would destroy their institute's charism. Others, however, believe ordination would complement their charism and expand their sisters' ministries.

Both outlooks—women religious distancing themselves from the clergy and women religious hoping for ordination—troubled the Roman Curia and a few bishops in the United States during the papacy of Benedict XVI. In late 2008 and early 2009, the Vatican announced twin investigations of women religious in the United States: the apostolic visitation of apostolic institutes within the United States; and the review by the Congregation for the Doctrine of the Faith of the Leadership Conference of Women Religious (LCWR). Both investigations ended after the election of Pope Francis.

Apostolic Visitation

The head of the apostolic visitation, Mother Mary Clare Millea, who was then the Rome-based superior of the Apostles of the Sacred Heart of Jesus, was asked to find funding for the evaluation of some 341 United States–based units of women's religious life, then comprising approximately fifty-seven thousand sisters. Cloistered nuns were not part of the review.

Her report of December 2014 was mostly positive. While the report noted the aging population of women religious (mid-to-late seventies), declining numbers, and fewer vocations, it emphasized the sisters' general respect for their elected superiors, their developed community life, and the prayer of the church. The institutes were lauded for their financial stewardship and their support of elderly members. For its part, the LCWR said the visitation reinforced the beliefs of various institutes:

> While the Vatican's decision to conduct an apostolic visitation caused great pain and anxiety for many Catholic sisters, our members frequently speak of how our experience of the study became the source of profound transformation for our institutes. The process led us to study the heart of our vocation as we engaged one another in significant conversations that explored our spirituality, our mission, our communal life, and our hopes for the future. As we did so, our bonds with one another grew even deeper and our understanding of the potential of this life to serve the needs of the world grew even keener.

The LCWR Investigation

The investigation of LCWR mandated by the Congregation for the Doctrine of the Faith concluded before the apostolic visitation. The "doctrinal assessment," as it was called, focused on three areas of concern to the congregation: its view that LCWR assemblies presented "problematic statements" and "doctrinal errors"; its view that LCWR members and officers expressed corporate dissent regarding women's ordination and the pastoral care of homosexual persons; and its view that LCWR espoused what the doctrinal congregation saw as "radical feminist themes" incompatible with Catholic teachings. The congregation's complaint also found LCWR "silent on the right to life," by which it meant abortion.

In April 2012, the Congregation for the Doctrine of the Faith ordered LCWR to revise its statutes to demonstrate that it adhered to "the teachings and discipline of the Church." The congregation appointed now-retired Seattle Archbishop J. Peter Sartain as overseer for up to five years, assisted by Bishop Leonard Blair, then of Toledo, Ohio, and Bishop Thomas John Paprocki of Springfield, Illinois, and an advisory team that, presumably, Sartain would name. (Note that none of the three prelates is a religious.)

Cardinal William Levada, an American and then-prefect of the doctrinal congregation, ordered that Archbishop Sartain have authority over LCWR especially regarding its statutes, plans and programs, use of liturgical texts, and affiliations with other organizations (especially NETWORK and the Resource Center for Religious Institutes). A few months later, in July 2012, Pope Benedict XVI appointed then-Bishop Gerhard Müller as doctrinal prefect.

Archbishop Sartain's mandate ended in 2015. Leadership of the doctrinal congregation and LCWR presented a joint report on the mandate's implementation.

The official niceties did not end the back-channel criticisms of women religious in ultraconservative social and other media, nor did it dampen episcopal support for newer, more conservative religious institutes of women, especially in the United States.

If anything, the combination of the two investigations solidified the view that the prophetic stance of women religious could only be lived outside the clerical system.

Nevertheless, members of the Amazon Synod in 2019 spoke forcefully about women deacons, both inside and outside the synod hall, noting that some two-thirds of parish groupings in the Amazon were managed by women, and predominantly women religious.

That fact alone speaks volumes about the Amazon, where the numbers of Catholics continue to decline. For example, a 2014 Pew Research Center survey found that 69 percent of the population in Latin America identified as Catholic, reduced from at least 90 percent in the 1960s. For the most part, younger, poorer, and less educated people have moved away from Catholicism to evangelical Protestantism and continue to do so.

Why? The so-called prosperity gospel is most attractive, or at least more attractive, to these former Catholics, especially those who are counted among the younger poor.

The question is not new. In 2018, Jesuit Fr. Antonio Spadaro and Pastor Marcelo Figueroa, editor of the Argentine edition of *L'Osservatore Romano*, wrote about the prosperity gospel in *La Civiltà Cattolica*, which Spadaro edits. The prosperity gospel, they wrote, "is used as a theological justification for economic neo-liberalism." While their article is widely seen as a rebuke to Trump administration policies in the United States, its concerns apply as well to the Amazon region, where clear-cutting, overgrazing, and the polluting of air and water are justified by a "prosperity" that promises to assist the poor.

As the prosperity gospel spreads around the world, how can women religious and women ordained as deacons challenge it? Perhaps not easily, but they clearly can. While it is increasingly decried, clericalism among Catholic clergy is an obvious shadow to the prosperity gospel, in terms of clerical "success" gauged by position, power, and money. In too many places and in too many cases around the world, clericalism is still an obvious part of the priestly class. The problem of clericalism is not new, but as it mirrors the promises of evangelical preachers, it presents a challenge to Catholic evangelization.

But women deacons are not priests, and women religious are particularly averse to careerism. Ordained or not, inside or outside the clerical caste, their ministries challenge the assumptions of the prosperity gospel and, coincidentally, the failures of clericalism.

FOR REFLECTION

1. How would having women ordained as deacons enhance the charism of your institute (or order)? How would your charism be lived out in diaconal ministry?

2. Prior to the pontificate of Francis, the Vatican began twin visitations of women religious in the United States: an apostolic visitation and a review of the Leadership Conference of Women Religious. How did these two events affect your institute? How did they impact you personally? Did these events strengthen your institute's charism and goals?

3. Women religious are still criticized in certain media outlets. Would diaconal ordination be helpful or hurtful to the way the public perceives women religious today?

4. In some parts of the world, including in the United States, the prosperity gospel has taken hold, especially in connection with clerics and clericalism. Would women religious ordained as deacons help dispel the connection? How can the abilities and witness of women religious counteract the negative impressions of the clergy?

5

Would the Ministry of Women Religious/ Women Deacons Benefit the Church?

Pope Francis's repeated calls for a "more incisive female presence" in church leadership have met uneven implementation around the world as well as at the Vatican. There are possible positions open to laypersons that might allow women—if appointed—to have a "more incisive presence" in the church. These are typically administrative positions and, at the Vatican at least, can be limited to five-year terms. (The assumption is that senior Vatican positions are filled by priests, who then return to their home dioceses.)

Again, women can be appointed to some positions, and women's viewpoints can make a difference, but only if they are considered. Depending on the Vatican office or diocesan structure, a woman is too often at risk of being ornamental and eliminated from actual decision-making.

Furthermore, it is important to recognize that calls for more women in positions of leadership are directed at only partial needs of the church. The "incisive presence" of women is also necessary in ministry—ministry to other women, surely, but also ministry to the poor and neglected of society for whom "church" is only a place to approach fearfully.

A painting that represents church in the time of Saint Francis of Assisi depicts the tragedy of his times. The rich and powerful, well-dressed, and educated are in the front, seated, watching a finely robed celebrant of a Mass. The poor and hungry, ill-dressed, and dirty are huddled in the back of the room, far from the celebration, and farther still from the church's ministry. The medieval church in which Saint Francis found himself was not one terribly interested in the poor, to whom he wanted to bring the gospel. He understood his charge was to "rebuild the church." He began with roof tiles and timber but ended with a ministerial revolution. Whether he was ordained or not, his desires were understood as diaconal.

Women have always been in the ecclesiastical "back rows." The discussion about women being restored to the ordained diaconate is not about their becoming clerics so they can invest their lives in clericalism, in the climbing, the money, and status and power. The discussion about women deacons has always been about ministry. It has been about ministry because the ministry of women—and the ministry of women deacons—is about the needs of the church. It is not about clerical power.

Throughout history, we see that the ministry of women deacons was often to other women. Women deacons ministered to women in baptism, they anointed sick and dying women, they catechized, and they gave spiritual direction to women, among their other ministries. At least, that is where the preponderance of historical evidence points. That was then. Who ministers to women now?

Clearly, the ministry of women religious has benefited the church for centuries. In many countries, women religious have built and staffed hospitals, schools, social service agencies, and homes for the aged and infirm. In mission territories, women religious brought the gospel to areas bereft of clergy and ministered to the social needs of the people.

Testimony about the work of women religious during the Amazon Synod certified the import of their ministry in the region. Would parishes and parish groupings in Amazonia—the majority of which are led by women and women religious—benefit from these women being ordained as deacons? Perhaps. Pope Francis's response to the synod's final document, *Querida Amazonia*, acknowledges the fact of women's leadership but separates it from ordination. Pope Francis seems to prefer the professionalization and canonical recognition of nonpriest parishes led by parish life coordinators (Can. 517 §2), be they laypersons—male or female, including religious—or deacons. So, it might not make any difference if a religious became a deacon.

In many cases, this is true, especially if the individual named as a parish life coordinator does not have a vocation to the diaconate. But it is disingenuous to argue that because a layperson can be named a parish life coordinator, there is no need for women to be ordained to the diaconate. For one, the parish life coordinator cannot preach during Mass. The benefit to the church, the people of God, if a woman—religious or secular—is ordained as deacon is that she becomes more clearly identified as acting and being in the image of Christ the servant as well as acting on behalf of the bishop.

The ordained deacon can have ordinary faculties for solemn baptism, witnessing marriages, and preaching. Only the most tortured routes through canon law allow bishops to grant laypersons, including parish life coordinators, these faculties. But the ordination of a woman as deacon is more than simply providing an easy way for women to baptize, witness marriages, and preach. Their ordinations give the people of God a direct conduit, if you will, to the ministry of the bishop. The woman deacon who baptizes does so in the name of the church; the deacon who witnesses marriage does the same; and the deacon who preaches at a Mass, technically, at least, represents the bishop.

The usual arguments apply here as well. The person who prepares an individual for baptism would then be the person who baptizes. Funeral rites led by the woman deacon who accompanied the dying individual, who witnessed the decedent's marriage or baptized his or her children, give solace to the family as well as to the parish.

There is no need to search for an either-or determination here. Individual parishes develop and grow as they will. If the woman religious who is already leading a parish finds within and without a call to the ordained diaconate, then she and the parish would benefit from her being able to live that call.

Deacons are clerics. But deacons are not, by definition, clerics on the rise. Religious, likewise, have given up the trappings of power and prestige in the name of service. So, a woman deacon who belongs to a religious community would proclaim her countercultural witness to the gospel in many ways. Her presence in the liturgy would symbolize her service and rootedness in Catholicism and its teachings. Her diaconal ordination would enable her service to the very people who most need to hear the gospel: the young, the poor, the uneducated. She would embody the call of the diaconate: ministry of the word, the liturgy, and charity.

FOR REFLECTION

1. Would the diaconal ordinations of women religious and other women help give women a "more incisive presence" in the church? If so, could they make a difference in church policy and procedure? What difference could this make on the diocesan and parish level?

2. Historically, women deacons ministered to women. Who ministers to women now? How could having women deacons affect the way the church ministers to women and how the church views and treats women in general?

3. Would women religious ordained as deacons be closer to the church of the poor or could their ordained status distance them from those in need? What effect could the presence of a woman religious serving within the liturgy have on the faithful?

4. Deacons are often thought of as ministering primarily to the social needs of the people of God. Would other ministerial tasks of women religious ordained as deacons be enhanced by their diaconal status?

5. The question of vocation is central to the discussion of women deacons. Would a woman religious serving in mission territories necessarily be better able to serve if ordained to the diaconate?

6. What prayer does this discussion inspire in you? As you engage these questions, in what ways is the Holy Spirit inspiring further action from you?

Contributors

Donna Ciangio, OP, DMin, is a member of the Sisters of Saint Dominic of Caldwell, New Jersey, and serves as chancellor of the Archdiocese of Newark. She served as international director of Renew International and director of pastoral services of the National Pastoral Life Center and is the author of several books for faith reflection, including *Advent: Waiting with Joy* (Renew, 2020).

Colleen Gibson, SSJ, is a member of the Sisters of Saint Joseph of Philadelphia. A founding member of the ministry team at the SSJ Neighborhood Center in Camden, New Jersey, she is presently a student at the Boston College School of Theology and Ministry. Her writing regularly appears in *Global Sisters Report*, *Give Us This Day*, and the *National Catholic Reporter*.

Irene Kelly, RSHM, is a member of the Eastern American Area of the Religious of the Sacred Heart of Mary ministering at the Beach Catholic Outreach in Long Beach, New York. An elementary school educator, she has cared for "boarder babies" at Bellevue Hospital in New York City and taught English as a Second Language at the RSHM Life Center, Sleepy Hollow, New York.

Phyllis Zagano, PhD, is senior research associate-in-residence and adjunct professor of religion at Hofstra University, Hempstead, New York. She belonged to the first Pontifical Commission for the Study of the Diaconate of Women. Her books include *Women: Icons of Christ* (Paulist Press, 2020) and *Women Deacons: Past, Present, Future* (Paulist Press, 2011).

Further Reading

Zagano, Phyllis. *Called to Serve: A Spirituality for Deacons*. Liguori, MO: Liguori Publications, 2004.

————. *Holy Saturday: An Argument for the Restoration of the Female Diaconate in the Catholic Church*. New York: Crossroad/Herder, 2000. (Spanish edition: *Sábado Santo*. Estella, Spain: Editorial Verbo Divino, 2018.)

————. *In the Image of Christ: On Being Catholic and Female*. Chicago: ACTA Publications, 2015.

————. *Just Catholic: The Future Is Now*. Melbourne, Australia: Garratt Publications, 2021.

————. *Women: Icons of Christ*. Mahwah, NJ: Paulist Press, 2020.

————. *Women & Catholicism: Gender, Communion and Authority*. New York: Palgrave-Macmillan, 2011.

————. *Women Deacons? Essays with Answers*. Collegeville, MN: Liturgical Press, 2016.

————. *Women in Ministry: Emerging Questions about the Diaconate*. Mahwah, NJ: Paulist Press, 2012. (Melbourne, Australia: John Garratt Publishing, 2012.)

Zagano, Phyllis, Gary Macy, and William T. Ditewig. *Women Deacons: Past, Present, Future*. Mahwah, NJ: Paulist Press, 2011. (Melbourne, Australia: John Garratt Publishing, 2012. French edition: *Des Femmes Diacres*. Toronto/Paris: Novalis/Novalis/Cerf, 2018. Spanish edition: *Mujeres Diáconos: Pasado, Presente, Futuro*. Mahwah, NJ: Paulist Press, 2019. Portuguese edition: *Mulheres Diáconos: Passado, Presente, Futuro*. Lisbon: Paulinas, 2019.)

Praise for
Women Religious, Women Deacons

"Once again, Phyllis Zagano, one of the leading experts on the history of the diaconate, has written a very provocative contribution engaging women religious and women deacons."

—Nuria Calduch-Benages, MHSFN, secretary of the
Pontifical Biblical Commission, professor and
director of biblical theology, Pontifical
Gregorian University, Rome

"Women deacons? Why? What would the Church and the world gain if this became true? What if some of these women deacons belonged to religious congregations? With solid facts and questions, Phyllis Zagano invites us to continue the reflection personally and to gather groups of men and women to continue the conversation, to widen our horizons, and to open our hearts to the promptings of the Holy Spirit."

—Carmen Sammut, SMNDA, superior general,
Missionary Sisters of Our Lady of Africa and
former president of the International Union of
Superiors General (UISG), Rome

"This timely work offers an engaging and thought-provoking response to the generative question, *What is the Spirit saying to the world church?* My best hope is that soon the book will find its way into the hands of able translators who will make it accessible to thousands of women religious and church leaders in the non–English-speaking world."

—Margaret Eletta Guider, OSF, chair of the
Ecclesiastical Faculty, Boston College
School of Theology and Ministry

"Restoring diaconal ordination to include vowed members of a religious institute raises significant issues worthy of further study. The gift within the pages of this small book are questions posed for reflection and discernment, questions valuable to leadership and to all members of the institute."

—Mary Hughes, OP, former prioress, Dominican Sisters
of Amityville, New York, and former president
of Leadership Conference of Women Religious

"Phyllis Zagano's book explores important questions related to the possible restoration of women deacons within the Catholic Church and raises various considerations about the relationship between the female diaconate and female religious life. The chapters are offered for reflective reading and discernment and will encourage individuals and groups to consider new ways in which women can minister within the church worldwide."

—Pat Murray, IBVM, executive secretary, International
Union of Superiors General (UISG), Rome